Koalas

Jill Esbaum

NATIONAL
GEOGRAPHIC
KiDS

WASHINGTON, D.C.

A koala!

These cuddly creatures are built for life in the trees.

Strong arms and legs? Check. Sharp claws? Yep. Good balance? You bet!

A thick, fuzzy coat keeps a koala cool on warm days and warm on chilly ones. Rain? Not a problem. This coat is waterproof!

The fur on a koala's rounded bottom grows extra thick, so even hard seats feel oh, so comfy.

Eucalyptus trees are everything to koalas— a place to hang out, grab some grub, or take a nap.

If a koala is awake and rested, it is eating, grooming, climbing ... or ambling along the ground to a different tree.

A koala spends *a lot* of its awake time plucking *a lot* of leathery leaves that need *a lot* of chewing. Most of the water a koala needs comes from the leaves, too.

If a koala gets tired of chewing, it stuffs the gloppy wad of leaves into its cheek to save for later.

Leaves, please!

fruit

bark

Many different kinds of eucalyptus trees grow in koala country. Each tastes different to a koala.

What tough food can you chew with your teeth?

Besides eucalyptus leaves, koalas will nibble the tree's buds, flowers, stems, and bark.

leaves

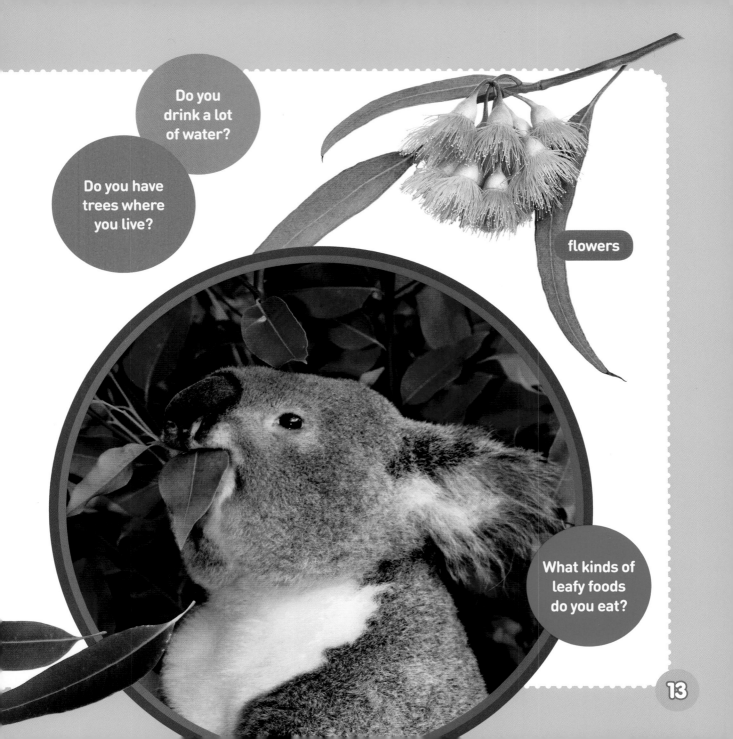

Do you drink a lot of water?

Do you have trees where you live?

flowers

What kinds of leafy foods do you eat?

13

A koala baby is called a joey. A newborn koala is as small as a bumblebee. Inside its mother's warm pouch a koala changes and grows.

Snuggle

Baby koalas have only one job: drink milk so they grow, grow, grow.

A mother koala hums to her joey. They talk to each other with soft clicks and squeaks.

Pocket protectors!

quokka

wallaby

Koalas are marsupials—animals that carry their babies in body pouches. While in the pouch, a baby grows bigger, stronger, and hairier.

Where do you curl up to sleep?

Do you like to be carried?

opossum

Pouches keep marsupial babies safe until they are big enough to live on their own. Other marsupials include kangaroos, Tasmanian devils, and most opossums.

What do you keep in your pockets?

Can you hop like a kangaroo?

kangaroo

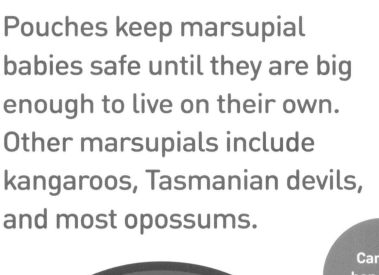

Tasmanian devil

G'day!

At about six months old, a brave joey begins leaving the pouch to practice moving around on its own. Reach and pull. Creep and crawl. Careful, junior!

Sooner or later, a joey wants a taste of leaves. Since it hasn't yet learned what its paws are for, it reaches with its mouth. Hold still, leaf!

When a joey feels tired, it slips back into the pouch for a nap.

23

One day the joey gets too big for the pouch! For the next year or two, the joey sticks close to Mom, learning to be a grown-up.

When the joey is old enough, it goes off to find its own trees. Koalas live alone, and each one needs about 100 trees all to itself.

Rub, rub, rub!

Each koala has its own territory, also called a home range. A male koala rubs its chest against a tree. The smell left behind tells other koalas that the tree is already claimed.

Koalas talk to their neighbors with booming bellows or loud, growly snores.

Sweet dreams

After a busy morning, there's nothing better than snoozing away a sunny afternoon. And snooze they do—for 18 to 20 hours of every day! Good night, koala.

Where Koalas Live

Koalas live in eastern Australia and islands nearby.

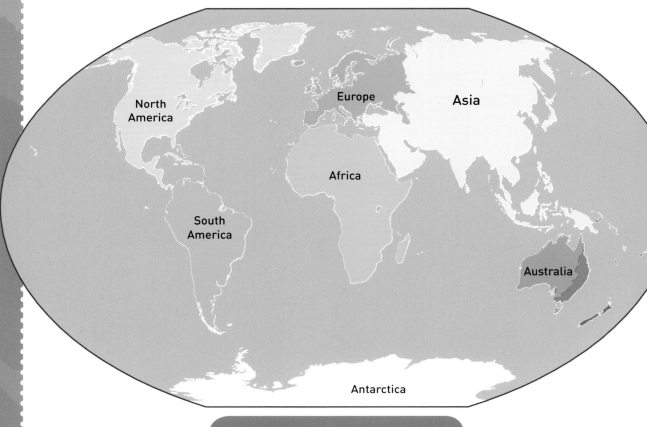

North America

Europe

Asia

Africa

South America

Australia

Antarctica

MAP KEY
☐ Where koalas live

Koala Maze

With your finger, show the hungry koala how to get to the yummy eucalyptus leaves.

For Dallas —JE

Editor: Ariane Szu-Tu
Art Director: Amanda Larsen
Photography Editor: Lori Epstein
Design Production Assistant: Sanjida Rashid

National Geographic supports K–12 educators with ELA Common Core Resources. Visit natgeoed.org/commoncore for more information.

Trade paperback ISBN: 978-1-4263-1877-1
Reinforced library binding ISBN: 978-1-4263-1878-8

The publisher gratefully acknowledges Dr. Bill Ellis of the University of Queensland's Koala Ecology Group and National Geographic's early education specialist Catherine Hughes for their expert review of the book.

PHOTOGRAPHY CREDITS

Cover, Suzi Eszterhas/Minden Pictures; back cover, ZSSD/Minden Pictures; 1, Steven David Miller/naturepl.com; 2–3, Mitsuaki Iwago/Minden Pictures; 4–5, blickwinkel/Alamy; 6, Gérard Lacz/Biosphoto; 7, imageBROKER/Alamy; 8 (UP), Jouan & Rius/naturepl.com; 8 (LO), Frank & Joyce Burek/Animals Animals/Earth Scenes; 9, Mitsuaki Iwago/Minden Pictures; 10, Ardea/Sailer, Steffen & Alexandra/Animals Animals/Earth Scenes; 11, Cyril Ruoso/Biosphoto; 12 (UP), Suzi Eszterhas/Minden Pictures; 12 (CTR LE), Archiwiz/Shutterstock; 12 (CTR RT), Robyn Mackenzie/Shutterstock; 12 (LO), Robyn Mackenzie/Shutterstock; 13 (UP), janaph/Shutterstock; 13 (LO), Miller, Steven David/Animals Animals/Earth Scenes; 14, Suzi Eszterhas/Minden Pictures; 16, Suzi Eszterhas/Minden Pictures; 17, Suzi Eszterhas/Minden Pictures; 18 (UP), Kevin Schafer/Minden Pictures; 18 (CTR), Danita Delimont/Gallo Images/Getty Images; 18 (LO), Cynthia Kidwell/Shutterstock; 19 (LE), Graham Melling/iStockphoto; 19 (RT), idiz/Shutterstock; 20, Suzi Eszterhas/Minden Pictures; 22 (UP), Robyn Mackenzie/Shutterstock; 22 (LO), Suzi Eszterhas/Minden Pictures; 23, Suzi Eszterhas/Minden Pictures; 24, Suzi Eszterhas/Minden Pictures; 26, Lacz, Gérard/Animals Animals/Earth Scenes; 27, blickwinkel/Alamy; 28–29, Cyril Ruoso/Biosphoto; 31 (UP), Gerry Pearce/Alamy; 31 (LO), arka38/Shutterstock; 32, Lacz, Gérard/Animals Animals/Earth Scenes; background (koalas), Rey Kamensky/Shutterstock; background (leaves), Aliaksei/Shutterstock; background (pawprints), elenkorn/Shutterstock

Printed in the United States of America
15/WOR/1